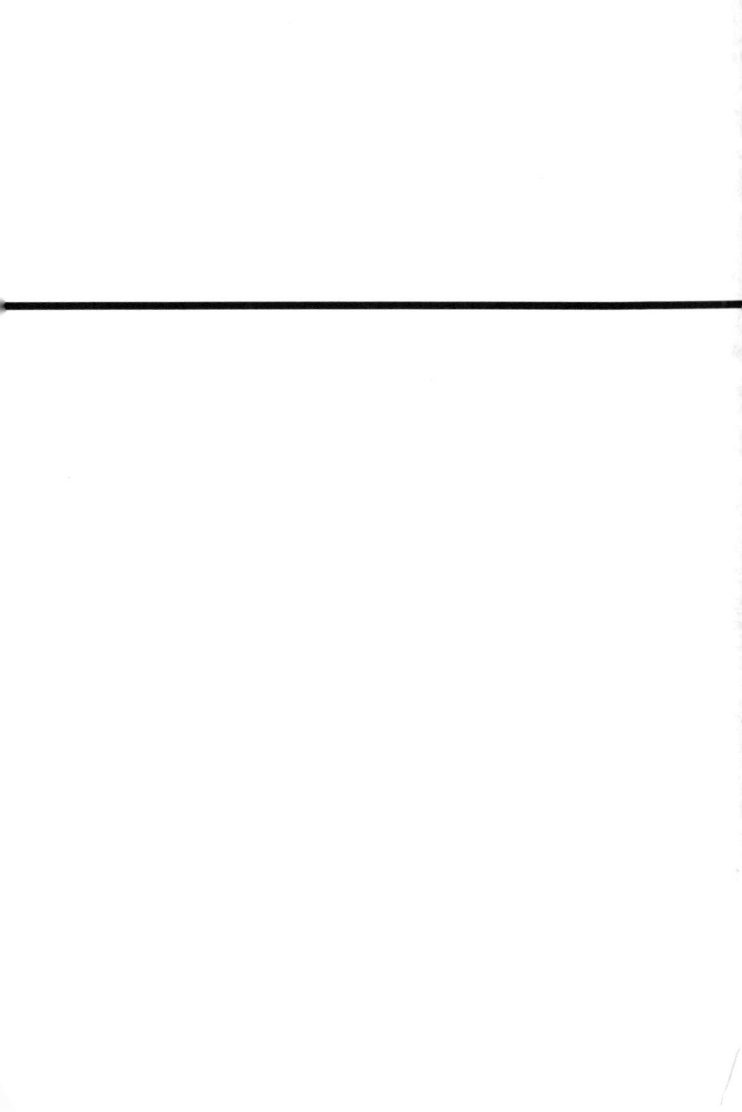

Holloway Crawl

Alex Blackbourn

Second edition published by Sixteen Books in London, January 2024.
First edition originally self-published in May 2023 by the author.
Please direct all enquiries to the publisher.

ISBN 978-1-7384951-0-8

Contents

I: Essay

Desire Paths and Holloways

A "desire path" is a route that has been visibly worn and clarified by persistent use over time, often contradicting existing or predetermined paths which are in these cases collectively rejected by the movement of people; an easily recognisable example of a common desire path is a shortcut across a corner of grass, as in fig. 1. It is the nature of space to influence movement within itself, even when this may conflict with a space's designed use by humans. Likewise, it is a characteristic of humans to mark and dictate the development of space, both intentionally and passively. The desire path exemplifies both of these qualities, becoming a collaboration between a community and its location, and evidencing the complex relationship between a space and those who occupy it.

When a path of any kind has been continuously worn over time, perhaps for hundreds of years and perhaps as a result of its wider significance, that path may become a "holloway", which is a reference to the trench-like "hollow way" that is dug through the earth and scars the landscape. As a concept, it is inherently linked to the desire path as again it demonstrates a sustained, mutually affecting relationship between humans and a space, and as such it is logical that a desire path may eventually become a holloway.

One of the original routes into London from Edinburgh and the North of England has been suggested to be an example of both a desire path and a holloway. As a cultural, financial and governmental centre for much of Britain's history over the last two millennia, the city of London has been visited frequently by people from all throughout the country, meaning that this route has been elected, heavily travelled and

Fig. 1. A desire path cutting the corner of a turning road.

developed into a holloway by both humans and cattle alike. Referred to in 1307 as "Le Holeweye in Iseldon" (Hidden London, 2023), the route went south and connected the villages north of London including Stroud, Tollington and the parish of Islington (Iseldon) until ultimately reaching the established city of London. By the 14th century an official road was built along the holloway by Edward III (Wittich, 1977), forming a part of what would be known as the Great North Road, the main route connecting London and Edinburgh for hundreds of years. This would later provide the basis of the modern day A1 motorway, serving the same purpose of connecting the North to London and still following the same exact section of road in North London that was once supposedly a holloway. That section of road is now referred to as Holloway Road.[1] I was among those funnelled by this route when I first drove into London from Yorkshire to move here in 2017; in the time since then, I have lived exclusively on Holloway Road or in its immediate surrounding area, Holloway. It has been the centre around which my adult life has indivisibly formed.

I am fascinated by these relationships between people and the spaces that they occupy, and more recently, the individual and collective relationships that communities form with urban spaces. This over time has materialised into a psychogeographic practice. Whilst it is important to recognise that the term psychogeography is incredibly fluid and has suffered many contradicting interpretations, my own psychogeography follows the study of exactly this relationship between people and space that is demonstrated so literally by Holloway Road. Though it is a complete coincidence that I have built up this practice whilst living in an area of great personal psychogeographic interest, for these reasons I am interested in developing a deeper understanding of both my local area, Holloway, and my own psychogeographic practice.

Thus, I present *Holloway Crawl*, a research project that seeks to holistically generate a psychogeographic picture of Holloway Road. More specifically, this research is designed to place the area's historical and contemporary cultural context, gathered through prompted research and archival exploration, against lived experiences of the road amassed from a series of walks I have taken along and around Holloway, collected oral histories and my personal history in the area. This autoethnographic, cross-sectional approach seeks to build a psychogeographic lens through which to examine the area, using these sources to flesh out the relationships between people and space as they have and continue to exist in Holloway, specifically within the research period of May to November 2022. The main initiator for this approach has been "dérive", or "drift", a practice of walking which is best understood in relation to psychogeography as the terms were coined at the same time, with and for each other.

---

1. It has alternatively been suggested by some that Holloway may have been named in reference to the general dip of the area between the hills in Highgate and the city as a result of water erosion. Others speculate a connection to the site's supposed use for pilgrimage, in which case Holloway would refer to "hallow", or "hallowed way". In any case, what we do know is that Holloway Road did not exist as a major route before at earliest the late 13th century due to the presence of the Great Hornsey Park, a large hunting ground (one of

Henry VIII's favourites) north of what is now known as Hampstead and Highgate belonging to the Bishop of London. The park's use as a hunting ground meant that regular commuters to and from the City were diverted eastwards around the park via Crouch End and Muswell Hill (Running the Northern Heights, 2023).

By the beginning of the next century, passage had been granted across this area for a toll, meaning that routes northward no longer had to sidestep the giant park, leaving the old north road redundant. This in turn led to the election of a new route which connected the City and Islington to the new road through Great Hornsey Park, collectively becoming part of the Great North Road. This inspired the establishment of Highgate, a connecting steep path down Highgate Hill and, most importantly, a new road which began southwards at its base: Holloway. There may well have been a previously existing trail along this route connecting the aforementioned villages in the area, but if so, it is during this time that its usage drastically increased and Holloway began its life as we know it.

I personally choose to believe that the formation of this specific section of the route might still have followed that of my desire path and carved-out holloway dreams, and I believe this is corroborated by the road's early history of recorded repair work. In the late 14th century, for example, after years of continuous traffic by humans and cattle alike, Holloway had become sunken and waterlogged, leading to Edward III contracting local hermits to build up and maintain the road (Wittich, 1977, p. 49). For me, these events acceptably correlate with what we'd expect during the of formation of a holloway.

Walking

Given by Guy Debord in his *Introduction to a Critique of Urban Geography* (1955, para. 2), the base definition for wider psychogeography is summarised as '...the study of the precise laws and specific effects of the geographical environment, consciously organized or not, on the emotions and behavior of individuals.' This definition is reflective of its context as beginning within The Situationist International (SI), an organisation of artists and activists based in 1950s Paris and devoted to 'The construction of situations [...] beyond the ruins of the modern spectacle' (*Report on the Construction of Situations and on the International Situationist Tendency's Conditions of Organization and Action*, Debord, 1957, para. 53). Influenced by both Marxist and surrealist philosophies, the situationists focused on alternate ways of perceiving time and space as to resist or reject the all-encompassing nature of capitalism within modern society. Situationist psychogeography at this point provides a methodology for engaging with specifically the city in ways that may lead to genuinely life-enriching experiences, and in this light the situationist focus on the environment's effect on humans – and less on the reverse – is clear.

Debord continues in *Theory of the Dérive* (1956, para. 3), writing that '...dérive includes both this letting-go and its necessary contradiction: the domination of psychogeographical variations by the knowledge and calculation of their possibilities.' To paraphrase, to dérive is to walk within a specific state, one that is aimless and drifting, drawn by the flow of the city and its terrain, whilst also holding a relevant contextual understanding in mind as to properly interpret the experience. For instance, if a desire path is evidence of a particular flow of people through a space, aimless wander may then lead the psychogeographer to encounter a path as such, whilst a maintained contextual awareness would allow them to identify this path and the conditions of the space that encouraged its development. It is through this walking-based practice that a specific, alternative experience and understanding of one's surroundings can be achieved. For the situationists, this meant moments of dissociation from the contemporary facts and realities of one's own surroundings as to momentarily escape the spectacle through 'situations'. This context in mind, Debordian dérive feels perhaps limited or restricted in comparison to later interpretations of psychogeography.

An important elaboration on the practice comes with the British movement of Psychogeography in the nineties and noughties; writer, poet and psychogeographer Iain Sinclair, for example, takes an approach that marks a significant departure from the SI's practices. Where to dérive in a Debordian way is to drift aimless, Sinclair would instead follow more structured and predetermined routes, the arbitrary gimmick of the walk providing the conditions for encounters to occur within. He exemplifies this in *London Orbital* (2003), which follows a series of walks that track London's ring road, the M25, narrating his journeys in first-person prose with observations and references. In this instance, the scope, the investment of time and the challenge of tracing the M25 offers *London Orbital* the means by which to become an original and intricate study of outer London, and thus the notion of gimmick widens the lens of dérive as it serves as a useful and alternative way of engaging with space to what comes initially or even instinctively – this is a particularly important factor to consider in the transition of scale from the SI's study of an entire city to a smaller, more specific area.

As one can imagine, exclusively wandering back-and-forth along a single road would not be a sustainable or fruitful study; here, gimmick offers an engaging solution. This manifested in the form of top-to-bottom walks of Holloway Road that similarly to Sinclair's were not strictly Debordian in that they followed a route. In turn, these organically led to the increasingly niche dérive gimmicks which eventually became the basis of my writing. As the area is one that I have lived in and am ultimately very familiar with, gimmick offered methods of engagement that cut across the patterns and routines that may have influenced my navigation of the space. In doing so, my personal psychogeographies attached to the area are not ignored, but rather subverted so that they can be made apparent, observed and articulated when necessary.

Inspired by The Situationist International's methodologies and incorporating elements of a contemporary British approach to psychogeography, these dérives remain a site for both knowledge production and data collection, and have been recorded in log-form throughout the research process. They serve also to prompt deeper research and exploration; whilst adamantly non-didactic in that they are not calibrated in relation to what I may expect or hope to find, they remain open to new, exposed threads of future research that may be found in a specified area. The notes from this process have since contributed to a piece of written prose which recounts and plots these walks against each other so that they are ordered spatially as opposed to chronologically, branching into further research when appropriate. This format, with its points of interest and narratives gathered organically through my aforementioned dérives, articulates a handful of the intrinsic connections and dynamics within Holloway that are crucial to a nuanced understanding of the area.

Writing

To briefly introduce autoethnography, I personally
appreciate the summary given by academic researchers Tony
E. Adams, Carolyn Ellis, and Stacy Holman Jones for their
chapter on autoethnography in *The International Encyclopedia
of Communication Research Methods* (2017, p. 1):

> 'Autoethnography is a research method that uses personal
> experience ("auto") to describe and interpret ("graphy")
> cultural texts, experiences, beliefs, and practices ("ethno").
> Autoethnographers believe that personal experience is infused
> with political/cultural norms and expectations, and they engage
> in rigorous self-reflection [...] in order to identify and interrogate
> the intersections between the self and social life.'

To connect autoethnography and psychogeography
explicitly, the notion of using personal experiences to construct
larger social understandings is already a recurring theme
in existing iterations of psychogeography, Iain Sinclair's
work being an inarguable example of exactly this. It is my
psychogeographic belief that the effect of a community on
the space it occupies is dealt not necessarily through larger
decisions and town planning, but rather in the day-to-day usage
of said space. For this reason, I am drawn to autoethnographic
research as a means to identify that daily communal dictation
of space through the collection of minute experiences, followed
by subsequent 'rigorous self-reflection' through recording,
writing and editing into prose. This is supported by the fact that
during these dérives the personal interactions that populated
these journeys genuinely felt like they would be valuable, even
if for reasons that were unclear at the time.

With this there is also a secondary value to these encounters as a way to illustrate the various micro-dynamics present, and by extension to render a holistic picture of an area; by this I refer to creative autoethnographic writing as a continuation of autoethnographic research. For Iain Sinclair, his specific use of prose succeeds in how it is anecdotal and personal, allowing his poetics to seep into the writing style and emulate some of the more intangible aspects of his experience for the reader, acting as a form of qualitative data in building a cultural understanding of London's surrounding areas. This writing style, and qualitative research in general, feels appropriate for the unquantifiable nature of cities. It is also important to distinguish that this is not at the expense of quantitative data – statistics and figures relating to Holloway may exist in the prose to help inform and contextualise the initial, experiential observations. In this way, autoethnography is again useful as a territory in which to develop the initial thoughts from these experiences through a writing process that integrates qualitative and quantitative data so that they are mutually supporting and critical of each other.

When making creative decisions referencing Iain Sinclair's practice, however, it must also be mentioned that a recurring theme with the aforementioned British movement is a tendency to nostalgically position the psychogeographic lens in relation to history, and I feel compelled to comment on this as it relates to my personal priorities as a psychogeographer. In *Psychogeography* (2006, p. 14), Merlin Coverley summarises this potentially problematic relationship to the past with his description of specifically Sinclair's perspective being one that '...views the present through the prism of the past'. Whilst I praise the romanticism of an approach like this, where does this style of writing leave the actual, often traumatic reality of a site in what presents as a fictionalised story of a place? What does this then mean for the relationship between the text and the present-day space in question?

Writer and Artist Laura Oldfield Ford here serves as a politically engaged alternative to Sinclair, her major autoethnographic work, *Savage Messiah* (2019), comprised of a series of zines self-released between 2005 and 2009 that collage writing, drawing and photography to create '...emotional maps...' (Watford Observer, 2009, para. 4) of London postcodes, '...chronicling a disappearing London, a lot of which has been completely erased for the 2012 Olympics', as she describes it. Oldfield Ford's subject is tethered to the history of a space in the same way a plant is intrinsically tethered to its seed, while the narratives she presents are inarguably current. The visible erasure – or uprooting – of these relevant histories are recorded in autoethnographic form over the course of her study and as a result there can be no allegation of her work being dissociated from the realities of its subject.

As a result of this, for my own methodology I am specifically interested in the histories that have a particular connection or interplay with the dynamics currently at work in the spaces I'm surveying; it feels important that this research is connected to the present in some way other than purely site. To address these concerns, I suggest that by prioritising the histories prompted by dérive, we are able to generate a nuanced picture of how these histories are layered into this space over time and have therefore shaped our experience today.

Drinking

As referred to in the title of this project, the following research has come to be structured around exclusively the pubs on Holloway Road. This decision was made in response to my research as pubs organically became central to my study throughout its course until they collectively offered a clear focus for the writing, which in itself is reflective of the cultural significance of pubs in what they reveal of the spaces around them.

Pubs occupy a unique cultural niche that is not matched by other businesses, nor other public-facing entities in a metropolitan area. As businesses, pubs must be successful to remain open, and thus are a way of gauging a community's engagement in an area over time – people "vote with their feet" so to speak. Unlike many other businesses, however, pubs are an optional place of leisure, meaning they reflect people's wants more than essentials such as supermarkets or banks, whilst also having to match the demands of a consumer's situation. Similarly, in the evenings they offer more of a social "third space" (a space to occupy outside of home or work) than other forms of hospitality such as restaurants, which often require a more substantial financial investment, or cafes, which tend to close outside of work hours. Though obviously there are exceptions and nuances to these trends, an establishment's long-term, continuous presence indicates that it matches at least some of the needs and desires of its local area, and by way of a capitalistic natural selection, pubs as an amenity in high concentration across relatively small subject areas can in this way be illustrative of these dynamics in a close, specific way. This is markedly the case for Holloway Road, where there is truly an abundance of pubs.

Because of this, whilst my initial dérives were numerous and varied, the majority of notes come from pub-oriented dérives later in the process with additional sections drawn from other dérives where relevant. However, before looking into these findings further, I'd like to step back and consider the ramifications of pub crawl as psychogeographic practice – becoming inebriated as part of a study opens up both ethical dilemmas and opportunities for fruitful research.

The idea of entering alternate consciousnesses for research purposes is immediately appealing in that it seems to disrupt the perceived formality and frigidity of academic practice. This is not an original sentiment, with Guy Debord himself engaging in such activities during the synthesis of psychogeography. Ian Marchant writes about this in his essay *Walking the Dog (For Those Who Don't Know How to Do It)* (2015, p. 50):

> 'Debord wrote that he came up with the term psychogeography when he was high on hashish and lost in a park. Debord and Wolman's first dérive through Paris was undertaken when they were very, very drunk. [...] The point is still, it seems to me, that the landscape is altered by consciousness, and that by altering our consciousness, we alter the landscape.'

When considered, a state of intoxication could in fact lend itself to the previously discussed aims of the situationists, to manufacture "situations" through which they are briefly able to escape the capitalistic spectacle.

However, this reasoning is initially concerning in that 'altering the landscape' seems to suggest a distorted view of reality, one that may be no more and perhaps even less tethered to reality than the unaltered consciousness. I would rationalise this by linking these ideas to Walter Benjamin's differentiation between 'optical' and 'tactical' understandings of space, which comes from an anecdote about architecture in his essay, *The Work of Art in the Age of Mechanical Reproduction* (2003, p. 120):

> 'Buildings are received in a twofold manner: by use and by perception. Or, better: tactilely and optically. Such reception cannot be understood in terms of the concentrated attention of a traveller before a famous building. [...] Tactile reception comes about not so much by way of attention as by way of habit. The latter largely determines even the optical reception of architecture, which spontaneously takes the form of casual noticing, rather than attentive observation.'

Here, Benjamin describes architecture as having two separate perceptions: one in the noticed, aesthetic experience of a building from initial visits or by briefly passing by; and secondly in the habitual, lived-in familiarity of a place where the aesthetic of one's surroundings comes secondary to the tactile, or felt. As a result of one's sustained familiarity of a space, one's experience of the space is altered and by extension they are minutely dissociated from the reality of their surroundings. Therefore, their operation within that space may too be affected, in particular over time as a space changes whilst their own internal and literal methods of engagement stay the same. With this in mind, altered consciousnesses may offer the means by which to move between these optical and tactile perceptions in the hopes of developing a more truthful picture of the "whole".

Benjamin also has the oft quoted 'To live means to leave traces' (*Reflections: Essays, Aphorisms, Autobiographical Writing*, 1985) attributed to him. In context he is referring mostly to interiors, but it is interesting to me to instead apply this thinking to urban spaces. This could obviously be considered literally, referring to how over time a space is marked and formed by its physical use – which would appeal directly to the concept of desire paths – but alternatively, we could also apply this to the slowly developed tactile reception of space; perhaps a requirement for the tactile experience of a space is not necessarily an investment of time but rather an accumulation of experiences to overwrite the visual facts of one's surroundings, the traces not literal but rather internally layered on the psyche.

It is essential for me to consider this effect on my lens as I study an area I have spent years living in; I am and have been actively participating in the subject of this ethnography, and thus my involvement with the space is unavoidably going to factor into my engagement. This thinking serves this research's nature as an autoethnographic study, which by definition involves the participation of the researcher in the context they are studying. Similarly, when looking at pubs it feels not just appropriate but essential to participate on some level as to avoid an uncomfortable subject versus spectator dynamic forming between myself as a researcher and the community I am living and working within.

While these reasons outline a convincing case for the pub crawl as a useful, uniquely revealing psychogeographic gimmick, there are genuine personal risks and dangers posed by this methodology that cannot be ignored. A psychogeographic practice that is based on alcohol consumption poses the risk of having serious health implications for the researcher over an extended period of time; it does not take critical analysis to know that binge drinking is not a good habit to get into, be it psychogeographic practice or not. Therefore, I feel a need to underline that whilst I believe that the pub crawl gimmick can be an effective and enriching method as part of a larger practice, in a larger sense it is not sustainable as the sole means by which to engage with an area, but rather as one tool among many to be used when appropriate.

Preamble

Before we begin the crawl, I would like to outline the format of the following text. Entries are ordered spatially according to the order of the pubs on Holloway road, starting from the top in Archway, and ending at the bottom by Highbury Corner. Because of this, many of the entries are presented out of chronological order, though each is dated for narrative purposes and to reflect the extended nature of this study. Dates annotated with (*) denote an entry written about a relevant visit outside of the research period. In each entry, if drinks were bought, their names and prices are listed. As previously touched upon, I could not come to any of these pubs blind – that is the nature of this research project given my history in the area – but I do also want to clarify that unless stated, the majority of any wider research around these pubs happened after the initial visit and during the writing process as I interpreted the notes from my crawls.

The time-frame of this research is an approximately six month period between late May and early November 2022. In the same way that it would be infeasible to adequately address every single facet of the history of Holloway Road, it is impossible to capture every aspect of life presently in Holloway, and as such it is not the design of this project to try and do so definitively. One example would be that not everyone in Holloway will drink alcohol, and so immediately the premise of this research is flawed and potentially skewed in this way. That being understood, I am still confident in the validity of this research as ultimately I was led by my experiences and research; I hope for it to offer a unique insight, though certainly under no pretense of being the only insight.

Holloway Crawl is designed so that with each pub there is space in which the reader is invited to record their own notes and observations, should they be inspired to attempt a crawl of their own along Holloway. I would suggest that any crawlers should not feel any pressure to record in a similar way to my own; there are countless forms that autoethnographic research can take, and I'm sure most of them are more interesting than mine. In any case, always crawl responsibly.

References

Online

- Anglesey, M. 2009. Artist Laura Oldfield Ford examines the legacy of new towns in Hatfield. *Watford Observer*. [Online] 25 November. [Accessed 11 October 2022] Available from: https://www.watfordobserver.co.uk/leisure/localexhibitions/4758619.artist-laura-oldfield-ford-examines-the-legacy-of-new-towns-in-hatfield/
- Debord, G. 1955. *Introduction to a Critique of Urban Geography*. [Online]. [Accessed 10 October 2022]. Available from: https://www.cddc.vt.edu/sionline/presitu/geography.html

- Debord, G. 1957. *Report on the Construction of Situations and on the International Situationist Tendency's Conditions of Organization and Action*. [Online]. [Accessed 10 October 2022]. Available from:https://www.cddc.vt.edu/sionline/si/report.html
- Debord, G. 1956. *Theory of the Dérive*. [Online]. [Accessed 10 October 2022]. Available from:https://www.cddc.vt.edu/sionline/si/theory.html
- Hidden London. 2022. *Archway, Islington*. [Online]. [Accessed 6 October 2022]. Available from:https://hidden-london.com/gazetteer/archway/
- Running the Northern Heights. 2023. *Holloway Road – History and Topography*. [Online]. [Accessed 19 December 2023]. Available from:https://runningthenorthernheights.wordpress.com/2021/05/23/holloway-road-history-and-topography/

Books

- Adams, T. E. et al. 2017. Autoethnography. In: Matthes, J. et al. eds. *The International Encyclopedia of Communication Research Methods*. New York, NY: John Wiley & Sons, Inc., p.1.
- Benjamin, W. 1985. Paris Capital of the Nineteenth Century. In: Jephcott, E. ed. *Reflections: Essays, Aphorisms, Autobiographical Writing*. New York, NY: Schocken Books, p.155.
- Benjamin, W. 2005. The work of art in the age of its technological reproducibility. In: Jenning, M. et al. eds. *Selected Writings, Volume 3: 1935-1938*. Cambridge, MA:Harvard University Press, p.120.
- Coverley, M. 2006. *Psychogeography*. Harpenden: Oldcastle Books, p.14.
- Ford, L. G. 2019. *Savage Messiah*. London: Verso Books.
- Marchant, I. 2015. Walking the Dog (For Those Who Don't Know How to Do It). In: Richardson, T. ed. *Walking Inside Out: Contemporary British Psychogeography*. London: Rowman & Littlefield International, Ltd., p.50.
- Sinclair, I. 2003. *London Orbital*. London: Penguin Books.
- Wittich, J. 1977. *Discovering: London Street Names*. Aylesbury: Shire Publications Ltd., p.49.

2: Crawl

12 June 2022
Alex: Islington Radio IPA (half pint)
Maggie: Goofyhoof Pacific Pale Ale (half pint)
Total: £6.40

At the top of a road that gradually but noticeably climbs an incline, The Archway Tavern seems to look over Holloway, and thus feels like an apt place to start. Inside it feels both very old and very new, the aged tile and cobble supporting a modern interior that is currently host to a man doing an afternoon DJ set on his laptop to a nearly empty room. The pub is somewhat famous for being the cover art of The Kinks' 1971 album *Muswell Hillbillies*[△] (The Kinks, 1971) which is framed and splayed on a wall in the corner. Today, our surroundings offer a sans serif interpretation of a pub such as the one pictured on *Muswell Hillbillies*, looking entirely dissimilar were it not for the windows. Our two half-pints cost over £6 together, and this feels telling of the pub that The Archway Tavern is today.

There is a welcome tiled into the floor of the entrance, 'Welcome to the Tram Bar', with the image of a Toucan sitting on the TFL Underground Archway sign beside a pint of Guinness. The branding matches that of the 'Guinness Time // Millennium Time' clock on the building's side which has seen better days (at the time of writing there are six letters left of the original sign, one of which is caught in a light fixture immediately below). This branding paired with the Gaelic typeface of the welcome seems to point to a history as an Irish pub, but there's also a feeling that the tavern has not been an Irish pub for some time.

The pub in its current form opened in August 2020 (Ferguson, 2020) with a major lick of paint applied after a period of nearly six years being shut. Prior to it being The Archway Tavern, the building spent some years as live music venue Dusk Till Dawn (Yelp, 2010), which in 2010 unsuccessfully attempted to become a strip club (Hussein, 2010). In 2014, the pub endured a failed stint as 'The Intrepid Fox' before going bust in March 2015 with a long, bizarre Facebook rant announcing their closure:

> 'You charge the freaky looking new guys 50% more rent, although they only have the room that holds 150 people, and stamp your foot like Rumpelstilskin when the water refuses to change to wine and the fuckin' Red Seas definitely do not part' (The Intrepid Fox, 2015).

Afterwards, the building remained closed for five years and was the subject of much public interest and debate. During this time the council rejected an application by the leaseholder to turn the building into a joint nursery and wine bar (Hotdinners, 2018) in an outrageous, aspirational appeal to Archway's yummy mummies.

The Archway Tavern having *at one point* been an Irish pub, however, is important to consider especially given the history of the Irish community in Archway, and this is reflected in the tavern's address on Navigator Square, the result of a £12.6 million pedestrianising redevelopment and renaming from 'Archway Close' in 2017 (TFL, 2017). After its completion, Archway's local community chose to honour its immigrants, voting for the new name, 'Navigator Square', as a reference to the term "navigator", or "navvies", used for the large group of Irish immigrants that moved to London in the early 19th century to build the city's canal system (Finch, 2017).

The entrance tile also makes reference to the public house being adjacent to an important interchange for trams, which would continue up to Highgate and down to the city until their closure in the early

1950s. It is presumably rails from these lines that are presently set into the floor of the pub between the cobblestones. The first ever cable tram in London began operating here in 1884 (Tramway Information, 2002), just four years before the public house's construction in 1888 (though there are records of two other public house buildings on this same site in the three centuries previous (Hidden London, 2022)). The building and trams are intrinsically linked also to the Hornsey Lane Bridge over Archway Road which was opened in 1900. These collectively highlight a period of substantial development in the area before the 20th century.

We sit outside with our posh pints and look over the road as we finalise the gimmick-centric methodology for our dérive.

> The methodology of this dérive will follow that of a "pub crawl", where my roommate Maggie and I will take a predetermined route, hopping from one pub to the next as to visit every pub on the road, drinking a half-pint of beer or cider at each place. Some may argue that in traditional pub crawl methodologies that a full-pint must be consumed instead of just a half, but to that I would roll my eyes. Additionally, if for whatever reason we do not want to stay for very long, we have pre-agreed that a shot of a spirit can be taken as a forfeit.

The pub lies in the shadow of Archway Tower – or Vantage Point as per its 2016 re-cladding and re-brand – which crowns the road and disfigures the skyline. The tower was the subject of a Ruth Ewan art piece *How to make Archway Tower disappear* (2012). A quote from this project I particularly like comes from an Archway resident, Fang, who after considering the tower's unpopularity with local residents suggests: 'I think it would be a good present to the people of Islington if we could make the tower disappear', and as such the art piece was a tower viewer showing a live feed of the view up towards Archway with the tower edited out. After years of sitting vacant, Vantage Point was "regenerated" by property developer Essential Living and today pet-friendly studio apartments start at £1900pcm (Essential Living, 2022).

Considering this with Navigator Square's coinciding rename, the later 2010s redevelopment of the square and the tower seem indicative of an anecdote about Archway shared by CSM tutor Anna Hart in a lecture I attended back in May 2022. Hart remarked how until recently Archway was seen as the 'edge of the successful city', referred to as 'upper Holloway' or 'lower Highgate' and rarely just Archway; apparently change from this is a relatively recent development. The council identifies the significance of The Archway Tavern in their *Islington Local Plan Strategic and development management policies September 2019* (Islington, 2019, p. 53), stating that 'Archway Tavern is a historic feature and a focal point of the Town Centre', suggesting that it should be considered the third in this holy trinity of Archway's recent discovery of identity. We finish our drinks and begin down the Holloway.

5 October 2022
Alex: Maple and salted caramel latte (tall)
Maggie: White chocolate mocha with soy milk (grande)
Total: £8.20

Though still bearing its original name and from afar looking very much like a pub, The Lion has been a Starbucks since 2016 (WhatPub, 2021). It is described as having once been a very Irish pub similar to The Archway Tavern, in recent history going by both Sweeneys' and O'Mara's. Swapping Irish for "Italian" in the present day, my Guinness substitute is far too sweet.

12 June 2022
Alex: Fosters (half pint)
Maggie: Strongbow (half pint)
Total: £4.10

We are greeted in the doorway by a notice of upcoming price increases due to 'Covid recovery' signed by the Phelan Family, the owners of this independent pub. It resembles a similar notice I came across last month, hung on the front of Green Jade, a Chinese takeaway further down Holloway Road (31 May 2022).

Due to inflation of ingredients,
we are forced to increase our prices by £1.00
ALL DISHES
SORRY, GREEN JADE

The act of notifying a customer base of price increases brings me to think about the chain-owned pub I previously worked at. That pub would automatically raise its beer prices on big rugby game days without notice, perhaps revealing a difference in the obligation to transparency these independent businesses feel that they must give to their customers, and by extension the relationships they must maintain with their local community to stay afloat.

Inside, The Mother Red Cap offers an immediate counterargument to The Archway Tavern and The Lion in how Irish pubs have survived in Holloway. A description by Tris C on pubsgalore.co.uk labels the establishment '...as resolutely Irish as they come' (Pubs Galore, 2017), which is corroborated by both the Irish flag emblazoned with a Celtic FC badge hanging outside and the elderly Irish accents arguing amicably with the bartender about who should be served first. Similarly to The Archway Tavern, this pub likely did not begin Irish; the diary of Samuel Pepys references a Mother Red Cap in Holloway on Tuesday 24 September 1661, which significantly pre-dates the main Irish migration to Archway in the late 19th Century.

> 'So we rode easily through, and only drinking at Holloway, at the sign of a woman with cakes in one hand and a pot of ale in the other, which did give good occasion of mirth, resembling her to the maid that served us, we got home very timely and well...' (*The Diary of Samuel Pepys, 2022, para. 1*).

The beer on tap is the standard pub selection, the place is attractive if slightly run down and it is busy but not overly loud. There is a jukebox and snooker table surrounded by gorgeous, wall-spanning mirrors on one side of the pub and a lone dartboard on the other. The staff are very kind to us and I notice Polaroid pictures of who I assume to be a mixture of staff and customers behind the bar. Two geezers behind us are trying to work out the name of an actor, moving through Harrison Ford and Marlon Brando before settling on and loudly cheering, 'GENE HACKMAN! YES!'

The Mother Red Cap seems unpretentious, but maybe this feels especially the case in comparison to the Archway Tavern, and for an almost £4 per pint average in London, we are very impressed. Despite only being a total of a pint down each, Maggie and I are already beginning to get emotional, stating how glad we are to be doing this together.

The Spoke

3 January 2022*
Alex: Americano (w/ oat milk)
Maggie: Americano (w/ oat milk)
Total: £7.00

Despite quite visibly occupying an old pub building, The Spoke has since 2014 been the type of bougie cafe where the filter coffee is more expensive than espresso-based drinks at £4.10 a cup, plus an extra 50p for alternative milks. They do actually have a couple of beers remaining on tap, though these are found at £6.50 a pint.

Having not been a pub since 2010 when it was known as Angie's (PubWiki, 2020), The Spoke's emphasis nowadays is very much on its cosy and homely vibe, a sentiment which is echoed on their website (The Spoke, 2022) and generally pleasant to experience in reality. However, as the name might suggest, they angle their business in part towards cyclists; this leaves an irrationally bitter taste in my mouth.

After ordering two (non-filter) coffees and while sharing a piece of lovely but accordingly expensive red velvet brownie, we dwarf this lavish investment by putting in a first offer for a flat we've just been to see on Archway Road. Though the excitement of the moment mutes the guttural shame of returning to London and paying these prices in posh, 'locally owned' bistros such as this one, I do not expect to return soon.

12 June 2022
Alex: Guinness (half pint)
Maggie: Guinness (half pint)
Total: £4.40

Currently in another Irish pub and not far at all from The Mother Red Cap, it is impossible to ignore the Irish influence on the area, which we toast with Guinness. I admit that I wanted to like this place before we came knowing that one of my favourite bands, Wolf Alice,△ made their start here, playing occasionally from 2010 onwards (Redmond, 2012). Although The Flóirín still holds regular live music (much of which is folk), Wolf Alice have not recently returned to perform here. Instead, later this month the band are playing the pyramid stage at Glastonbury, which I suppose would be a marginal upgrade in some people's minds.

Inside it feels slightly stagnant, the room livened only by a few voices and the sound of golf from the televisions punctuating the room. By the other customers of the pub – a family and a few pool-playing older men – we feel a bit watched. Perhaps this is not a space for us, and that would be okay. Nevertheless, the Irish landlady is lovely to us and we enjoy our drinks on the road-facing outside tables.

From the outside, we observe that The Flóirín sits slightly awkwardly in its place on the road, seemingly pulling in its shoulders as if it were on a crammed tube. This speaks to the pub's solitary position on the corner of Whittington Park, bordered only by grass and road. It is evident that The Flóirín once capped a row of terraced buildings facing Holloway, but these have since made way for the grassy mounds that front the park, looked over by a painted mural to the park's titular Dick

Whittington and cat which decorates the side of the pub. Guarding the entrance gap between these mounds is also a large shrubbery sculpture of the same cat, and behind the left mound is the Cromwell Road WW1 memorial plaque, placed there in 1994 (London Remembers, 2022). What this site does not commemorate, however, is Harambee House. (In the interest of transparency, the following information was uncovered whilst working on a separate archival project in April, sourced mostly from documents in the George Padmore Institute archive (Harambee, *The Harambee Project, 1969*). I include it here as it reveals both a necessary aspect of the road's history, as well as what first drew me to archival research.)

In 1969, Brother Herman Edwards, an Antiguan bricklayer and later social worker, founded 'Harambee', or 'Harambee House', in an old Butcher's building at 571 Holloway Road. Harambee was created to directly address the needs of the time as primarily a hostel, offering a place to stay for disenfranchised Black teens in North London. Harambee also offered various forms of cultural education and support: among other things, this included a regular film programme showing pivotal Black films such as *Reggae* by Horace Ové (1971) and *End of the Dialogue (Phelandaba)*(Caccia & Louvish, 1970), help for residents applying to jobs and reaching out to those potentially looking to hire, and free advice from lawyers every Saturday in relation to insurance, passports or legal troubles. Not only was Harambee vitally important as a hostel, but it also became a cultural hub in Islington which supported its community in a range of different ways. The ethos of this project is summarised succinctly in Reverend Wilfred D. Wood's 1978 written testimony to the project: 'Harambee's philosophy is simple. No person will ever be written off.'

This project was beautifully but contentiously documented by photographer Colin Jones for an article in The Sunday Times Magazine: 'ON THE EDGE OF THE GHETTO: The way they see it' (Gilman & Jones, 1973), who later toured the country in 1977 with photographs from this series, referring to Harambee and the series as *The Black House*. Brother Herman objected to this name, assumedly as this drew a false equivocation with Michael X's 'Black House' (see House of Hammerton, p. 74), with which Herman had briefly been associated with, but in reality was wholly unrelated to Harambee. Similarly, Jones' tour was controversial for the success he was garnering – or exploiting – from a community that was barely making ends meet. This disparity is made particularly apparent when considering the resistance Harambee faced from Islington Council at the same time and throughout the decade.

Being awarded a sum of £281,000 by the Home Office in 1973 to officially purchase the Holloway Road property and officially registering as a charity in 1976, Harambee seemed to be gaining rightful governmental validation and support for their work in Holloway. However, this funding was blocked by Islington Council, who on their Home Office-mandated requirement to provide 25% of the total amount withheld the full grant on the stipulation that the property instead be bought by the council and then rented to Harambee for a 'nominal fee'. Given the rising support for the National Front at the time and a very reasonable desire for financial autonomy, Brother Herman refused, stating that the money had been awarded to Harambee and that relinquishing the lease to the council would not be to the benefit of the project, nor its residents. Despite the Home Office agreeing that the prerequisite was unnecessary and even contacting the council to request that they release the funds, Harambee had still not received any portion of this grant by 1975. In 1978, after five years of negotiation and subsequent court battles with Islington's Labour council, Edwards was forced to officially decline the funding and instead rely entirely on donations. In the same year, Harambee experienced a 'fire incident' and was forced to make a desperate plea for local support.

From archival material is not clear how long Harambee lasted after this point, but no material is present from after 1978. Similarly, it's not clear what happened to the £281,000 either, other than it being a drop in the pond of around £2 million of public funds allegedly unaccounted for by Islington Council during the 70s. At some point soon after, the row of houses including 571 Holloway Road were demolished to make way for the front of Whittington Park, which, as mentioned before, memorialises the semi-fictional London Mayor Dick Whittington and his almost certainly fictional cat. They are present in the park's name, its painted mural adorning The Flóirín, its large scale shrubbery sculpture slash guard-cat, the local hospital (Whittington Hospital) and another, smaller, cage-bound sculpture of the cat at the bottom of Highgate Hill. This supposedly marks the exact point at which Whittington heard the Bow Bells calling him back on his departure from London for him to turn around and become London Mayor.

At the time of writing, Harambee House is afforded none of the same legacy, existing only in letters, posters, and leaflets kept by the George Padmore Institute on Blackstock Road, the collective consciousness of the local people that may remember it and in the awkward posture of a pub it once sat in file with.

△ One of the photographs taken by Colin Jones shows a group of young boys in front of a sound-system with the logo of 'Sir Fanso the Tropical Downbeat'. Sir Fanso was the figurehead of a sound popular in North London at the time, playing artists such as Alton Ellis and Slim Smith on Holloway Road at the 77 Club among other places across Finsbury Park and Tottenham (Reel, 1981). Further information about the 77 Club on Holloway Road is elusive.

Chris Stevens Ltd.

Chris Stevens Ltd., a large trade discount centre, sits in a building with a facade that references its history as The Norfolk Arms, a Whitbread's Ales pub 'proudly' rebuilt in 1900 AD but closed as a pub in 2003 (PubWiki, 2003).

Whilst walking past in 2017 on the way to the CSM campus on Elthorne Road, there was a student on my foundation who recommended I shop here for work boots and high-visibility jackets. When we talk about middle class creatives fetishising and appropriating working class aesthetics and culture, this serves as an excruciatingly direct example. I later once saw them at uni wearing a hard hat.

The Crown

12 June 2022
Alex: Strongbow (half pint)
Maggie: Strongbow (half pint)
Total: £4.40

As far as we can tell, the Crown is not an Irish pub, as is perhaps suggested by its monarchy-referencing name. There are both Irish flags and shamrock-bearing flags for St Patrick's Day, but these are accompanied by English, Scottish, Welsh, Italian and French flags, presumably for the 2022 Six Nations tournament, which is odd considering Six Nations and St Patrick's Day were both in March.

Otherwise, with an aged customer base – one of whom making a hilarious comment about Maggie (a woman!) buying the drinks – our experience of The Crown is a bit depressing. It overwhelmingly feels like we are a couple decades short of the target demographic and, as in cases before, that is okay; there are plenty of places for us. We drink quickly whilst admiring an old dog free-roaming the pub, slowly greeting each of its guests, and we discuss our strategy of avoiding the toilet for as long as we can so as to not "break the seal".

31 May 2022

At 596 Holloway Road is, or was, Nambucca, a once legendary music venue that often hosted the likes of the aforementioned Wolf Alice, Florence + The Machine and Pete Doherty's Babyshambles△ during his occasional periods of exile from The Libertines. I went once in 2017, seeing three bands that were not very big and unfortunately aren't much bigger now, but the Glaswegians who travelled for the support act were fun and we were given free beer.

Throughout the noughties Nambucca was one site of the UK's at-the-time flourishing nu-folk scene, exemplified by the nigh-resident Frank Turner, Beans On Toast, Marcus Mumford of soon-to-be Mumford & Sons fame and Laura Marling,△ who was here when she began her career at 16. One handy thing for us about this particular brand of descriptive, autobiographical song writing is that it paints a clear picture of what this scene was like, or at least of how its participants wanted to mythologise themselves. In his song 'The Pub in Holloway' (*Standing on a Chair*, 2009), for example, Beans On Toast describes this community and music culture that had formed around the pub as it met its demise with a fire in 2008.

> 'Well Andy lost his passport and university degree
> Danny lost his laptop and Rainbow lost her tree
> Ally lost his bedroom and Jamie lost his job
> Mike Russell didn't own much but he's still pretty pissed off
> North London lost a boozer, a venue and a stage
> And everyone will really miss that pub in Holloway
>
> All the things we lost in the fire
> All the things we learned on the way

Is this the end of an era or just a pub in Holloway?
It started in the basement on the 18th of December

And now all that's left are memories we can't remember
The band lost their equipment and they went their separate ways
It's pretty safe to say that things will never be the same
But it came with a brand new year a time for change and that
I'd like to thank Alan Pownall for lending me his flat'

Frank Turner describes this same culture and name-checks the pub in
'The Ballad of Me and My Friends' (*Campfire Punkrock*, 2007).

'The musicians who lack the friends to form a band are singer-
songwriters
The rest of us are DJs or official club photographers
And tonight I'm playing another Nambucca show
So I'm going through my phonebook, texting everyone I know'

Despite Nambucca being rebuilt and ultimately surviving the 2008
fire, a few weeks ago the venue had to close permanently due to lack
of business, largely because of Covid. 'The Ballad of Me and My
Friends' was the last song in Frank Turner's headline set for the pub's
final ever gig on the 13th of this month (setlist.fm, 2022). Somewhat
unfortunately for Nambucca the rest of the song is desperately corny,
though I'm sure it was well-received on the night.

In the door frame is an open can of Red Stripe, placed seemingly in
tribute. The window is occupied by a poster of a man wearing a shirt
that reads, 'SUPPORT YOUR LOCAL MUSIC VENUE'.

12 June 2022
Alex: Mangoliscious (half pint)
Maggie: Mangoliscious (half pint)
Total: £6.10

The Owl & The Hitchhiker for us begins with a brief conversation with the bartender after bonding over our shared Northern pronunciation of 'sun' (he's from Bradford, I'm from Beverley). I tell him about how I'm doing a pub crawl for research, prompting him to share an insight about one of the later pubs on Holloway Road, Flynn's; it's our next pub and needless to say we're excited.

The bartender also reveals the Owl & Hitchhiker's history as another Irish pub, with its original whisky signs still remaining above each of the windows. The building has its original name, The Half Moon, carved into its exterior facade, having also been known in the last twenty years as both The Edward Lear and The Quays, the latter of which being run for 16 years by Galway-born Finbar Holian (Graty, 2010) before being bought in 2016 by a firm from Buckinghamshire (Inge, 2016). Since then, however, the pub has re-branded under a new name through Laine's ownership, a brewing company and pub franchise from Brighton.

Part of this rebrand is an apparent desire to appeal to quirky 20-somethings, its own website describing the pub as 'funky' (Owl & Hitchhiker, 2022) while offering life-drawing classes, retro arcade games in the back and a broad vegan menu. It's clearly trying to be fun and Instagrammable, though this seems sad when it's as quiet as it is. There's a Progress Pride flag hung proudly behind the bar, and with it comes the unfortunate fact that one of the most outwardly socially progressive pubs on the street is also one of its more expensive, which feels in keeping with its parent company's origin in Brighton. That being said, there are far more expensive pubs on this road.

Despite its proximity to various student accommodations, it is apparent that the target demographic is slightly older than that, leaning more towards early-career professionals and yuppie families, this fact being reflected in its committed but poorly-maintained 90s video game aesthetic (only one of the four controllers at our table being functional). While at first this feels perhaps oddly placed this far up on the Holloway, this may be reflective of the demographic as you move towards Tufnell Park, Kentish Town and Highbury.

4 June 2022

It is the Queen's Platinum Jubilee weekend. Walking past Flynn's and absent-mindedly peeking through the window, I see it populated with the rowdiest group of pensioners I've ever seen. The walls are seemingly floor to ceiling with as many Union Flags as they can fit, and loud big band music gyrates the aged but unhampered crowd. I continue on, perplexed and impressed.

12 June 2022
Alex: Tequila shot
Maggie: Tequila shot
Total: £6.20

Flynn's Public House was first introduced to us by the bartender at Owl & The Hitchhiker, who recounted having gone in and being offered meat to purchase from a ziplock bag. Similarly, he described an interaction he witnessed where someone had put in a request with the meat man for some Arsenal themed bed sheets, to which he responded by returning twenty minutes later with the sheets, selling them for a tenner haggled down from £25. Aside from meat and homeware it's also apparently a good place to buy drugs.

This in hindsight is a fittingly inexplicable introduction to a pub that sells itself on its website as bringing a '...cosmopolitan flair to a traditional setting' (Flynn's Holloway, 2022). Unless they are referring to class A narcotics, it's hard to identify exactly what this 'cosmopolitan flair' might be past the Cafe Nero-chic framed arrangements on the walls and an obnoxiously loud DJ.

The crowd is mixed though leaning elderly, maintaining a buzz that is equal parts cheerful and volatile. After skipping around puddles in the toilets, I get us each a forfeit shot of tequila and we leave, unfortunately meatless.

24 September 2022
Alex: Fosters (pint)
Maggie: Hercules Smooth (half pint)
Total: £6.00

In the time since our last visit, the Flynn's Public House we knew before has shut and re-opened as The Hercules, marking a return to the original name shared by its adjoining road. The interior's radical makeover is hard to pin down – think Irish pub meets gentleman's club meets shabby-chic saloon meets small town antique centre. Maggie is a big fan. Little of the pub's 'cosmopolitan flair' remains, but a bronze plaque to 'JEAN QUEEN OF HOLLOWAY' has survived on one of the dividers.

The new owners, True Pub Co, pride themselves on their website as being a '...small collection of pubs founded on traditional values...' (True Pub Co, 2022). Via some table signage there is a plea for Instagram users to 'Snap a shot of our RETRO Guinness pump', making sure to tag The Hercules in any posts.

Asking the bartender about my surprisingly cheap pint, he tells me the £4 Fosters goes up a quid when the live music comes on and that apparently it was £3.90 pre-renovation. Even with the hike, it is still one of the cheapest pubs on the road. 'It's not lost its core clientele,' remarks Maggie, 'which seems to be prehistoric.' As if summoned, Russell approaches.

Russell, who has been drinking at The Hercules for 48 years, has told Maggie that she has a 'million pound smile'. He is as confused as I am about the revamp with its newly distressed wooden floors, ringing true with his statement that they 'did it up just to do it down again'.

Picking up on my accent, he tells me of his brother who moved north so that his wife (an 'expensive cow', as he describes) could have horses. I unwisely reveal that Maggie is also a horse girl and Russell, true-to-form, brands her as my assumed wife an expensive cow also. After trying and failing to convince him that you can in fact have a job at a gallery these days, we wish sweet Russell our goodbyes, but not before he gives Maggie a kiss on the wrist and myself a strong handshake.

31 May 2022

The Nags Head Morrisons acts somewhat as an divider between two separate factions of the road's supermarkets. Discounting the Tescos, Sainsbury's and off-licences which are distributed evenly, there is a trend in which the three Waitroses occupy lower Holloway on the south side of the Morrisons, whereas then the three "budget" supermarkets – Lidl, Iceland, and Aldi – hold the north. While it would be brazen to interpret supermarket placement as definitively indicative of all that much, opinions draw themselves about a section of road that requires three successive Waitroses. On this note, it's then interesting to speculate on the motivations behind closing the Nags Head M&S in 2018 to move it up to Navigator Square in Archway, especially considering Archway's coinciding redevelopment (Islington Gazette, 2018).

18 August 2022

As I pass through the Holloway end of Seven Sisters Road known as Nags Head, it is bustling. There is a diverse selection of independent off-licences, butchers' and grocers' among other stores, almost all of which seem to be busy. In an oral testimony given for Rowan Arts' *Making Inroads* (2010, p. 70), Nags Head local (and one time resident of Harambee House) Desmond Riley notes the area's changes since the 70s: 'Now the shops have got colour. They didn't know about colour then, it was grey and white. It's only since the influx of other cultures that's really shown England what a difference colour can make to the community and to the area.' Scattered amongst these shops are a selection of chain stores and fast-food establishments, and stretched above the Betfred and its neighbouring Mightypound hangs a long sign for an independent professional snooker club, Cousins.

The 2019 Islington Local Plan identifies there to be four 'town centres' in Islington, each '...a focal point for commercial, cultural and civic activity in the borough' (Islington, 2019, p. 130). Nags Head, one of the four, is geographically the point at which the three others, Archway, Angel and Finsbury Park, meet. Because of this, it is tempting to consider Nags Head as the focal point of Holloway Road and even perhaps Islington, especially with its nature as an intersection and transitional space palpable in the experience of the space. Discussion of "flow" often feels overly abstract when overused in psychogeography, but in the case of Nags Head I do think it's an appropriate concept to apply to the overlapping channels of people that meet at this intersection. There is a very real feeling of two streams colliding that impacts your movement within the space, and resultantly Nags Head is a difficult place to stay still. In the imagined centre of these streams, at the top left corner of Seven Sisters Road, lies Merkur Slots, a casino, in the structure of which you can just about recognise the remains of what was once a public house; until 2004, this was The Nag's Head (PubWiki, 2021). In a testament to the cultural weight of pubs and the way culture is canonised in London, the area's name, which is assumed also by its market and shopping centre, is a reference to a pub that hasn't existed for almost twenty years. The casino faces Admiral, another casino, and a McDonald's.

The pub's current occupants reflect the economic hardships experienced by the area's largely working-class demographic over the last thirty years or so, be that recession, austerity, a pandemic or a brutal combination of the three. Islington Council comments on this also in their local plan where they refer to the building's use as a casino: 'The unit is symbolic of the challenges faced in Nag's

Head with a concentration of pawnbrokers, betting shops and money lenders.' This 'concentration' of betting shops and adult gaming centres is immediately apparent, particularly at the end of Seven Sisters Road where there is a casino directly opposite another, separate casino. This analysis by the local plan in relation to Nags Head's 'challenges' may be somewhat explained by a 2021 study at the University of Bristol which suggests that 'Betting shops in the UK tend to 'cluster' in areas where people can least afford to gamble and some argue that this is a deliberate strategy of betting companies who are targeting the most vulnerable' (Evans J. and Cross, K., p. 5).

As I continue across Holloway and along Tufnell Park Road, the experience differs drastically from that of Nags Head. After an initial area of council housing, Tufnell Park Road quickly becomes very quiet, very residential and very middle class, an indicator of which being the Tufnell Park Tavern, which advertises beer, BBQ, and petanque. There is no semblance of the community as it exists on Seven Sisters and it feels like a wholly unrelated London on the west side of Holloway, separated by far more than a road and around 500 metres. The division that is created by the A1 is again mentioned by the local plan, describing Holloway Road as '...a heavily trafficked route which creates a major barrier dividing the Town Centre. The amount and speed of traffic creates an unsafe environment for pedestrians' (Islington, 2019, p. 45); perhaps this is an explanation for the assumed cultural divide also. This interpretation would seem to articulate Holloway as a fixed dividing line that presently separates the posh north-west of London in Highgate, Hampstead and Kentish Town from the historically more economically disadvantaged north-east in Finsbury Park, Wood Green, Tottenham and Walthamstow.

5 September 2022
Big Red Pilsner (pint) and a Big Red Shot
Total: £8.20

At 20:36, I order what will be my last pint of the night at Big Red, a dive bar adjacent to a student accommodation in which I lived two years ago. I never came here then, mostly because of Covid. The metal music playing (currently 'Toxicity'△ by System of a Down (*Toxicity*, Malakian et al., 2002)) is jarring against what is a mostly empty bar, but it is comfortably dark and plentiful with corners in which to crawl, all seeming to compliment the mohawk-baring pool players in the back. Two bartenders, one of whom off-duty with a pint, are complaining about the price of drinks elsewhere in London, which I feel is justified considering how cheap it is here; their £3.50 Bud Lite is the cheapest non-Spoons pint I've seen on Holloway.

By quarter past nine I've made friends with a loud but friendly middle-aged Canadian, Sheldon, who is currently visiting London to see the new ABBA show as part of a multi-part cross-european adventure. Once I have a £4 Big Red Shot (cranberry juice, peach schnapps, and Jäger), I steal one of Sheldon's cigarettes and vacate the premises.

25 September 2022
Alex (+3 others): Big Red Pilsner (4-pint pitcher)
Total: £12.00

Sitting at a booth in Big Red, a woman approaches us and asks for a pound for food. Before I can apologise for not having any cash on me, the bartender inserts himself between the woman and myself with his back to me. The bouncer then arrives also, and she is soon forced out of the pub. As she leaves, the bartender turns back to us.

'Sorry guys, welcome to Holloway!'

9 November 2022
Big Red Pilsner (pint)
Total: £4.40

Big Red is bouncing, and whilst it's unclear whether this solely because of it being a game day or not, there are more than a few Arsenal shirts about. One big difference between Big Red and the other pubs visited on this dérive is the apparent gender split – there is a considerably higher proportion of women here, which perhaps indicates something about the ways in which safe-spaces have formed along Holloway, especially in relation to the often toxic culture of British football. As with the Owl & The Hitchhiker, there is a Progress Pride flag hung behind the bar; I am reassured to know that a public declaration of a space's allyship does not necessarily have to come at the expense of its cheap drinks.

The vibe is very healthy. As I finish my pint, a woman in an Arsenal top comes to the bar and orders a round of shots for her table. They are completely unaware of this.

Taco Bell

19 July 2022

Across the way, I see evidence of another closed pub in the remaining parapet for The Old Kings Head, cruelly upstaged by the American branding of a Taco Bell that popped up earlier this year. The Old Kings Head ceased as an entertainment venue in 2011 when it was hideously titled as The Gaff (WhatPub, 2021), which had itself been rebranded from its original name at some point between 2008 and 2010. When I first moved to Holloway it was a Costa Coffee, and not once did I ever visit.

† *In memoriam: As of July 2023 the Taco Bell on Holloway Road is closed. While it is satisfying to watch Holloway spit up and refuse to absorb any American chain, I doubt they will be too disheartened with branches in Finsbury Park and Camden remaining open and assumedly popular.*

22 June 1983*

Soon to close permanently, a double bill of *Blade Runner* and *Body Heat* is the last thing to show at the ex-ABC cinema now known as The Coronet (Cinema Treasures, 2022).

> '[Deckard does some amazing climbing, then jumps to next building. Roy follows, holding a white pigeon.]
>
> Roy: Quite an experience to live in fear, isn't it? That's what it is to be a slave.
>
> [Deckard spits at Roy as he falls; Roy catches him with one hand.]
>
> Roy: I've seen things you people wouldn't believe. Attack ships on fire off the shoulder of Orion. I watched C-beams glitter in the darkness at Tannhauser Gate. All those moments will be lost in time like tears in rain. Time to die.
>
> [Bird flies off...]' (Scott, 1982).

22 June 1986*

From the balcony stalls at New World Snooker Club (stagedoor, 2010), the faint sound of balls clicking together can be heard from below in the main auditorium, which is separated by a low faux ceiling. This is accompanied by the sound of 2p mounds falling in the amusement arcade machines that occupy the foyer. The balcony section is unused by humans, left to decay and inhabited by pigeons – perhaps they enjoy the abundant cigarette smoke.

A white pigeon has made a nest in one of the abandoned seats. Someone in the auditorium below begins a new game, breaking loudly.

[Bird flies off…]

5 September 2022
Stowford Press Mixed Berries (pint)
Total: £2.29 (supposed to be £1.99)

The Coronet JD Wetherspoon is an art deco ex-theatre which was in 1994 converted into a pub, becoming an iconic fixture of Holloway Road's terrain. It is a particularly great spot for people-watching. In response to an evidently new member of staff receiving abuse from demanding customers, an older bartender mediates whilst another defends the newbie angrily; it is easy to imagine how a place like this can quickly feel like a battlefield. The newbie ends up charging me for the wrong pint but I do not correct her (what is 30p really?) and she compliments my nail polish. A middle-aged man at the bar grieves to his friend, 'This country's the worst; everything's on its knees.'

This Spoons is slightly cheaper than The White Swan at the bottom of Holloway Road, and is often perceived to be one of the cheaper Wetherspoons in London. User jadeisrlycool vouches for this in the most-liked comment on aprilxwinters' TikTok video, *The 5 best Wetherspoons in london from a broke bitch n spoons veteran x* (2022): 'The coronet in Holloway is the cheapest spoons I've ever been to! £2.99 double rum and coke'.

Taking a standing table in the centre of the front area, I observe my surroundings. It's busy, but as an old theatre building its regal high ceilings make the room far quieter than it would be at similar occupancies elsewhere. The crowd is a varied mix of old and young and there are at least three different languages being spoken in my earshot, accompanied by a chant of 'Mashallah! Mashallah! Mashallah!' which is moving through the room. Behind me, two old men are sitting talking whilst a third at the next table over stares at them intensely. In the opposite corner, two men sit with evidence of eight pints of Guinness between them, four of which untouched. I love ambition.

Its reputation as a JD Wetherspoon precedes it, but the popularity of The Coronet and the position it takes on Holloway Road cannot be denied or ignored. In his article for The Observer, *How Britain fell for Wetherspoon's* (2017, para. 4), journalist and Holloway native Ed Cumming illustrates this:

> 'Who doesn't like Wetherspoon's? Watching my local, the Coronet on Holloway Road, over the course of a week, it's hard to know. Certainly not the students, who pile in to get leathered on the cheap. Nor the Arsenal fans, for whom pre- and post-game pints are as ritual as their club's underperformance. Not the families with young children, taking advantage of the pub's child-friendly early evenings. Not the early-afternoon men who nurse silent pints alone at high tables. Not the two women in their 20s, waiting for their friend to pop to the loo before they start snogging in front of a jug of orange cocktail. Not Margaret Veal, in her 70s, originally from Ireland, who comes every week with her partner after dancing.
>
> "It's the only place that's like pubs used to be," she tells me.'

9 November 2022
Stowford Press (half)
Total: £1.20

Arriving at The Coronet at 19:45, there are two bouncers outside on the door, and inside are another two. This atypical security presence immediately demonstrates this crawl's niche – it is an Arsenal game day, which offers a version of Holloway Road that would be wrong to miss. Arsenal, who play at the Emirates Stadium not more than a 15 minute walk away as per a proud sign behind the bar, are playing Brighton in a third round League Cup fixture. This match-up does not offer particularly high-stakes, with most Arsenal fans focused mainly on their current 1st place position in the Premier League, but knock-out matches between two premier league sides as such can be special. Brighton are also playing well this season despite having lost their season-starting manager Graham Potter to Chelsea, and there is a somewhat interesting, somewhat artificial rivalry being manufactured between Brighton and Arsenal by the sportscasting forces that be. The game began just before I got here.

After receiving an unsettlingly cheap half-pint in a plastic glass, I sit and begin my usual process. By default, Wetherspoons very rarely show football and tonight is no exception, meaning most avid fans are elsewhere, but in their absence I feel an interesting environment facilitated by said vacuum.

There is a man on a table near me eagerly making a point of speaking to each of the staff members that pass him. He mentions that he is from Eritrea to one trapped bartender who absolutely did not ask, but is nevertheless receiving the information graciously. Many of the staff are wearing Arsenal shirts, including one that has 'BOSS LADY 1' plastered across the back of her shirt. I'm a big fan of that. The building is not very busy at all, and after doing a quick scan I decide to leave, though not before a table of lads give me a 'right on brother' in their best deep south American accent (for context, I've recently cut myself a mullet à la Billy Ray Cyrus).

9 November 2022
Staropramen (pint)
Total: £1 (with food)

Getting back to the Wetherspoons over an hour after I left, the crowd is essentially unchanged. I make the decision to eat and wait for the trickle of fans from the stadium after the game finishes. When my food arrives, Brighton goes 2-1 up, and my pint later follows, split between two plastic chalices. By 21:42, Brighton has won 3-1.

Within 15 minutes, Arsenal fans have begun to filter in amongst chants of 'WE. ARE. TOP OF THE LEAGUE. WE ARE TOP OF THE LEAGUE.'(† *In May 2023, Arsenal's 1-0 loss to Nottingham Forest thanks to a 19th minute effort from Taiwo Awoniyi officially awarded the 2022/23 Premier League title to Manchester City. So close!*) Another example of misery avoidance comes with a man a few tables over from me.

'No extra fixtures in February, who gives a fuck?'

Soon the Coronet is bursting at its seams, and there is evidently little that could dampen this crowd's mood.

† *(In memoriam)*

1 January 2023*

While we eat our breakfasts wordlessly in a booth at The Coronet, New Year's Day has brought a warm hum to the space which unfortunately falters before our table. A sombre awkwardness sits uncomfortably with the grease in our tender, punished stomachs. Harvey cuts the silence stupidly, admirably, and most of us at least expel through our noses. Already, amongst that of liquid Lurpak and watered down orange juice, we've a taste of what's to come this year, and it is going to be a long one.

26 November 2023*

It is a Sunday and I am desperate to get the most out of a day. Wanting to exchange a broken pair of Apple headphones at the Holloway Argos (for a third time, no less), I realise I have arrived too early and the catalogue store is not yet open for business. I have just over half an hour before it does, and I'm hungry. A natural solution reveals itself.

Sleepily, the lone drinkers sip and speak softly. The traditional breakfast I order at the till, which I enjoy as always, accompanies a hushed conversation on the phone with my mum, with whom I have plenty to talk about. It is a beautiful pub and an especially lovely place to be in the morning when crisp light pours through its tall windows, spotlighting the room's ornate decoration and sullied pews; at this holy time, the space feels more like a church than a pub or a theatre, albeit one that smells like stale beer and bacon fat.

However, when I leave, I do so briskly, neglecting the opportunity to observe any moment of prayer. I have not seen any of the articles saying that The Coronet had found a buyer back in August (Marsh, 2023a), and I know nothing of the pub's soon to be confirmed closure on 10 December 2023 (Marsh, 2023b). I exit without a second glance, leaving for the last time.

I was informed about The Coronet's permanent closure on 10 December 2023 thanks to a TikTok (samd_official, 2023). In the article announcing this closure, the new proprietors declare their intention to bring back The Coronet as a public house, but still I feel less than hopeful. In the time since releasing Holloway Crawl, I have been asked many times what the "best" pub on the road is, and I have always struggled to answer that question; how do you quantify the things that qualify one pub as better than another? Generally, I find that most meet a different need and are the "best" at whatever that is. But the most essential to Holloway as a whole, and by extension the most essentially Holloway? That has to be The Coronet. It was for anyone.

Knowing that the pub was put up for sale in November last year (Oluwalana, 2022), in the original edition of Holloway Crawl I remark my cynicism for whatever takes its place being able to meet the needs and wants of its local community as The Coronet does, or did. Since then, with this dangling sword of gentrifyocles hanging above, there certainly has been an abstract feeling that no singular loss of an establishment on the road would mark it more. I hope I am wrong.

5 September 2022
Carling (pint)
Total: £4.20

Feeling it an inappropriate place to order just a single half
pint for whatever stupid machismo-related reason, I order a
full Carling at a decent price and sit in a booth adjacent to the
group of four men currently occupying the bar and debating
heatedly. One of these men is the bartender and is currently
drinking with the group. Another man is separately on the
bandit in the corner, evidently quite drunk. A BT poster has a
sticker over the faces of Tottenham players Heung-Min Son
and Lucas Moura. There's a Sporting Limerick shirt signed
by the full squad on the wall opposite a Brazil shirt signed by
Pelé. UB40 and Chrissie Hynde's version of 'I Got You Babe'△
(*Baggariddim*, 1985) plays on the speaker.

The toilets are separated by Islington Sports Bar & Grill's
definitions of gender: 'Players' and 'Golden Girls', whilst a
third bears the graphic of a man playing wheelchair basketball.
Inside, the stickers on various surfaces tell a story of various
conflicts and points of contention within the Arsenal fanbase.
One calls for 'Justice For The Archway One', an Arsenal fan
who was banned from the stadium for a '...non-football-related
incident' (Morris, 2016). Justice was eventually awarded to
Mick Doherty, the banned fan, having his ban reduced by a
year in time for the 2016 season, his appeal supported by none
other than Islington MP Jeremy Corbyn. On another sticker,
the Hampshire Gooners declare their position against AFTV
(Arsenal Fan TV) for the violent offences committed by regular
host Mr DT against women (O'Brien, 2022): 'DT, SHE SAID
NO!'.

As I leave, the outside stretch of pavement is particularly vibrant with life as a large group of elderly men talk around a bench beside a late-night barber's.

9 November 2022
Carling (pint)
Total: £4.80

Passing through a raised security presence once more, I enter a desolate Islington Sports Bar dwarfed by a giant-size England flag on its front-facing exterior. Assumedly for streaming rights related reasons, the game is not showing here either and instead the Man City-Chelsea game is on. Again in a plastic glass, I receive a price-inflated pint of Carling and perch centrally in the room, unclear as to whether the price increase is game day-related or because the bar is just more expensive now. I'm not sure exactly what I was expecting, but considering I had such a positive opinion about it here last time, I feel slightly let down. However, while the vibe is sedentary, it is warmed by the bouncers and bar staff joking with their regulars.

As I leave and pass Fireaway Pizza on the way to the stadium, I notice its occupation by half a dozen police officers, standing docile but presumably ready to scuttle back to the riot van parked opposite upon receiving their orders, be those Neopolitan or Metropolitan. This presence extends through to the start of Hornsey Road which leads up to the stadium. Evidence of crowds lies with each of the overflowing bins and the soft roar emanating from the sold out, Camden Hells-sponsored Emirates ahead. I pass a woman on her phone, catching from her conversation, '...oh do you think I'm scared of a taser?'

Whilst in the impressively soundproofed Emirates gift shop, I miss both sides scoring to make it 1-1.

5 September 2022
Alex: Pravha (half pint)
Maggie: Pravha (half pint)
Total: £9.80

Deciding to return to Big Red and The Coronet later in the night as they are open the latest, we continue to Arkstar, a new-ish pub underneath one of the railway arches by Holloway Road underground station. Its name is a combination of "Arch", as per its location, and Telstar△(*The Original Telstar: The Sounds of the Tornadoes*, 1962), the popular 1960s hit performed by The Tornados, written and produced by Joe Meek up at 305 Holloway Road, who is famous for the song, his obsession with trying to speak with the dead and for ultimately shooting his landlady and then himself.

The crawl is beginning to get messy, initially not noticing the ridiculous amount charged for these half pints. At the next pub it will become clear that we'd been charged double and we won't have time to return and rectify the situation.

In the past I've had little reason to even notice Arkstar other than seeing it overflowing with red and white shirts on game days, which is unsurprising given its closeness to the Emirates. Today is not a game day however, and it is very quiet. Considering that the pint should be £4.90, it's not too bad for London, I know I've paid significantly more for Pravha before, but I also wouldn't call it cheap. Otherwise, the vibes aren't bad, tepid perhaps – this pub just does not inspire strong feelings. I think it would be better to return on a game day to get a more rounded experience of the establishment. We drink quickly to make it to the next pubs before they close and in hindsight, this feels like the beginning of the end for us.

9 November 2022
Pravha (half pint)
Total: £2.45

Another security check later, this time with a friendly but full-body frisk, and after an interaction with the bartender in which I replied 'And yourself!' to his 'Enjoy your pint!', I sit down and attempt to make out the highlights and scores from possibly the grainiest television on Holloway. The road's glass ban continues with this plastic half, and I drink quickly, gaining very little from this empty establishment and the indie muzak it's playing.

Just as I leave, a man unsubtly points at my head and says laughingly to his girlfriend, 'shall I do my hair like that?'

---

† *In memoriam: Arkstar closed in January 2023, citing Covid and governmental blunders as making it impossible to stay open in their Facebook goodbye. They also thanked fans of the Arsenal.*

31 May 2022

At 205 Holloway Road is the Victoria Tavern. The pub has remained the same since I lived here in 2018, but this appears to be an anomaly having previously found itself in a particularly tumultuous period of failed businesses, changed names and even a period of squatting in protest of rent prices (Finch, 2017). This apparent steadying of the ship and return to original name comes from their franchise ownership by Frontier pubs, which as of 2019 is owned by the Stonegate Pub Company, the largest pub company in the UK.

I have a personal history with the pub as it's one of the few places this end of Holloway you can rely on to have the football showing. After watching Liverpool's stellar comeback against Barcelona in the Champions League semi-final here in 2019, the Victoria became a lucky spot for myself and some Liverpool supporting friends. That was until the Champions League final against Real Madrid last week, but we'll leave that there.

12 June 2022
Alex: Brixton Atlantic APA (half pint)
Maggie: Brixton Atlantic APA (half pint)
Total: £5.90

We reach Victoria Tavern just as they're beginning to wind down and as one may expect, they're empty. I'm a bit concerned by the beer selection in that there's nothing particularly cheap, and the Victoria Tavern's partnership with Flatboys, a pizza chain that operates specifically within pubs, is equally menacing with its pizzas starting at £7, or £9.50 if you want cheese. They're playing Soccer Aid 2022 on a large projector screen to an empty room and the toilets are considerably nicer than those at Flynn's. We speak with the bartender and the manager about us being overcharged at Arkstar and they get very upset about this mistake, perhaps even moreso than ourselves.

9 November 2022

Unexpectedly, they won't let me into the Victoria Tavern as I don't have a ticket to tonight's game, but this is fine with me as I literally cannot see a single customer inside as I peek around doorman. Making my way back up the road, it's around half time, it's still 1-1 and a match steward is currently in the queue for Kacey's Chicken.[△]

[△] Kacey's Chicken became a site of pilgrimage for me after hosting an episode of Amelia Dimoldenberg's *Chicken Shop Date* (2022) in April, featuring international superstar icon and personal hero Charli XCX. The thought of Charli finding herself on Holloway Road sparks immense joy for me.

5 September 2022
Amstel (half-pint)
Total: £2.50

Making the assumption that the cheapest pint here is Amstel, I order half a pint at a very fine price. There are several groups in at the moment, some eating, but the pub could fit more than a few more, and as such it feels quieter than it is. The single bartender is eating a portion of chips behind the bar.

The interior feels slightly like a saloon with its all wooden floors, surfaces and walls and the 70s disco music playing in the background, though any old-fashioned mystique is somewhat broken by the pub being card only. It is an odd pub that is charming if not totally exhilarating.

Whilst crossing the road on the way to the next pub, I overhear a conversation between two men.

'Trust me sir: Jesus is up there, believe it or not!'

'I totally get that... I am a Christian.'

The Lamb

12 June 2022
Alex: Guinness (pint)
Maggie: Water (pint)
Total: £5.20

The Lamb is not a bad place for what will be our last drink.
I take a full pint in a feeble attempt to continue the dérive
under some suggestion that I'll 'drink for the both of us' at this
one, but Maggie's gaunt expression as we sit down clarifies
that this will be the final stop. Whilst she rushes off to find a
toilet to tactically expel into, I take the moment to soak up the
surprisingly vibrant Sunday vibe. The crowd is of mixed ages,
there's a seven piece Irish band playing in the corner and the
bartenders are cool and intimidating.

Not long after, Maggie returns and we leave, making it across
the road to just behind the bus-stop, where we sit and look
back on the last few pints we've had. This is literal, as Maggie
has returned them to the world, laying in the foetal position
on a bench. It is entertaining to watch the passersby traverse
Holloway Road's most recent bench-to-curb stream, regardless
of the two women that call us disgusting as they hop the River
Maggie. An hour and a bottle of water later, we board one of
the passing 43s or 263s to get home and I internally commit to
being wary of this dérive methodology in the future.

Polite Reminder: When crawling Holloway Road – or
anywhere for that matter – it is crucial to line your stomach
(which is something Maggie now preaches). Luckily,
Holloway Road is rich with places to do just that. The
following are my personal favourite food options at the time
of writing, not including Spoons.

Che Cosa, Italian, 653 Holloway Road
Nid Ting Thai, Thai, 533 Holloway Road
LahmaCino, Mediterranean / Turkish, 530 Holloway Road
Azuma, Japanese, 361 Holloway Road
Kacey's, chicken shop, 223 Holloway Road
The Hope Workers Cafe, proper caff, 111 Holloway Road

5 September 2022
Signature Brew Studio Lager Pilsner (pint)
Total: £4.80

The Lamb is unfortunately without an Irish band this time.
Inside, the bartender is sympathetic to the desperation in my
eyes as I ask her for the cheapest lager they have on draft,
which at £4.80 could be worse for this end of the road.

As with last time, both bartenders are cool and intimidating;
today's crowd, however, are mostly 20s and 30s young
professionals, talking about their five-a-side leagues among
other things. Each table has a central candle, and in the window
they are advertising a Met Gala-themed fancy dress event
hosted by The Lamb to which tickets are £20. Emblazoned
on the back of a t-shirt worn by a woman near me is a
message that feels explicitly revealing of the pub's millennial
demographic.

GOOD SEX
NO STRESS
ONE BOO
NO EX
SMALL CIRCLE
BIG CHECKS

31 May 2022

At 95-97 Holloway Road is House of Hammerton, a microbrewery that states, 'Our passion is delivering a beer that can be enjoyed by the many, not the few' (Hammerton, 2017, para. 1). This vapid interpolation of Labour's 2017 manifesto (The Labour Party, 2017) is telling of the assumedly left-wing customer base that the brewery's position within Jeremy Corbyn's constituency must hold, but this is also funny to me as here is where I was first introduced to London's golden new age of full pint-priced two-third pints (or "schooners") in 2018. The main reason for my interest in the building, however, comes from some recent archival research I did concerning an unrelated hostel project further up Holloway Road (see The Flóirín, p. 40) which brought me also to this building's history.

The 'Black House' was a Black Power commune and supposed cultural centre, supermarket and restaurant run by the controversial Michael X (known also as Michael de Freitas, or Michael Abdul Malik) during the 1970s. I use the term 'supposed', as the Black House ultimately never officially opened, despite the amount of funding it allegedly received via '...heavy guilt trips, targeting white radicals, saying they should donate as a way as a form of reparation for the crimes of slavery' (Darkest London, 2013). Michael X's handling of funds and operation of the house was often contentious, climaxing with an incident in which businessman Marvin Brown was invited to the house, beaten and then made to wear an original slave collar whilst being walked around the room after failing to pay a black employee wages that he had promised him (a moment very inaccurately depicted near the beginning of Roger Donaldson's film *The Bank Job* (2008)).

Though jailed, Michael was released on bail (paid for by John Lennon, no less) before fleeing to Trinidad and ultimately being hanged for his involvement in a pair of murders. The house, on the other hand, closed and was subsequently burned down in 1970. None of this is reflected in the current building as perhaps you may expect, but it is interesting to note how it remains a site where cash is bled from rich young liberals, albeit under drastically different circumstances.

12 June 2022

As we reach the next pub, House of Hammerton, they're closing slightly early. Whilst we're disheartened that we now can't finish the pub crawl tonight, we accept this without protest. I wouldn't want to be working right now either.

5 September 2022

This time it's a Monday, and House of Hammerton is again closed. I interpret this as a sign that I don't need to come here again; I'm in no rush to take out the mortgage required of pints here.

8 September 2022

At just about 18:30, while riding the 43 bus southwards down Holloway Road, I pass House of Hammerton and refresh Twitter on my phone. The Queen is dead.

October 2018*

BIRD sits against the multiple other chicken shops on Holloway Road in that the chicken is served on waffles, with syrup and slightly stale. My mother and sister are visiting me to see how I'm getting on at my new place just up a few doors from here, but currently they are fawning over the man waiting our table. He is charming and gorgeous to be fair.

While running the nearly empty restaurant to its close, a man comes to the front door. Upon seeing him, our waiter rushes to the back and emerges moments later with a large white bag, which he hands over with a warm 'here you go mate'. This moment reads like a regular happening.

31 May 2022

BIRD has since 2016 occupied a pub assumedly once called The Castle as is hinted by its lasting signage, but on BIRD's arrival it had been left empty for a year following the closure of its previous tenant, a pub called The Bailey (PubWiki, 2022). Aside from the incorporated ex-signage, the restaurant is a prime example of the archetypical, aggressively approachable London chain with a well paid graphic design team.

† *In memoriam: As of January 2023, BIRD Islington is closed. Unlike with Arkstar (p. 86), there is no post by BIRD on Facebook (or elsewhere) to thank their local community and hosts.*

The Famous Cock

12 June 2022
Alex: Pilsner Urquell (half-pint)
Maggie: Pilsner Urquell (half-pint)
Total: £6.50

There is a pretty rancid vibe as this Sunday is pulling slowly to a close. It's dead save for a few straggler students, and a pub like this has no right being this pricey. It feels like something between The Crown and Victoria Tavern; Stonegate operated and evidently Dunelm inspired, it is a sad, expensive alternative to the Wetherspoons next door. Perhaps I am being too harsh, but we are just not in the mood for this cock, famous or otherwise. I end up finishing Maggie's half as she clearly has hit a wall.

△ The Famous Cock's long side faces The Garage, a music venue at 20-22 Highbury Corner. There is a plaque to the band Orbital, who played their first ever gig here in March 1990 when the venue was briefly known as Town & Country II (London Remembers, 2023). More recently, the 2021 Ukrainian Eurovision contestants, Go_A, played here later in the month after this entry (The Garage, 2022). It is one of only two regular music venues remaining on the road, the other being The Grace, which shares the same building and offers smaller gigs in a more pub-adjacent setting. Both are owned by the music venue management company, DHP Family (DHP Family, 2023).

The White Swan

5 September 2022
Alex: Worthington's Creamflow (half pint)
Total: £1.00

At 18:40, I arrive early to eat first as I'm eager to avoid Maggie's pitfall on the last dérive, and the food here is cheap. There's a table of rowdy students near me, but aside from this and a few other anomalies, most of the room are older men, the luckier of which (but far from the majority) are in groups of two or three, amongst which there are also a handful of women. A table near me is having an impassioned conversation with some chest touching; are they arguing? Are they about to fight? Are they expressing love? A third arrives and an abundance of pointing fails to clarify the situation, but either way it seems relatively harmless and inexplicably in slow-motion. Encounters like this give the room a healthy buzz.

Later, a man comes round with a backpack full of bacon and salmon, offering the Co-op branded packages to drinkers at 3 for £5, or 6 for £10. No one questions this. With a man just behind me who made the mistake of showing some interest he bargains: 'Come on give me the twenty I'll give you the ten back, this is expensive stuff', before expressing a gentle 'I love ya man' when the man relents and buys £10 worth of mixed meat. Once he finishes his Stella, he wraps the bacon and salmon in his newspaper and leaves with it. At 19:05, I get my half pint for a single pound because of a 'Monday Club' deal, and even the bartender remarks to his colleague about the cost. I haven't had Worthington's before. Somehow, I feel as though I still may have overpaid.

References

- Aprilxwinters. 2022. *The 5 best Wetherspoons in london from a broke bitch n spoons veteran x*. [Online]. [6 October 2022]. Available from: https://www.tiktok.com/@aprilxwinters/video/7141431491380251910?_r=1&_t=8WE65Fbg2q5&is_from_webapp=v1&item_id=7141431491380251910

- *Blade Runner*. 1982. [Film]. Ridley Scott. dir. USA: The Ladd Company, Shaw Brother, and Blade Runner Partnership.

- Bonno, S. 1985. I Got You Babe. Hynde, C. and UB40. *Baggariddim*. [Digital]. Birmingham: DEP International.

- Cinema Treasures. 2022. *Coronet Cinema*. [Online]. [Accessed 6 October 2022]. Available from:http://cinematreasures.org/theaters/4301

- Cross, K. and Evans, J. 2021. *THE GEOGRAPHY OF GAMBLING PREMISES IN BRITAIN*. [Online]. Bristol: University of Bristol, Personal Finance Research Centre. [Accessed 6 October 2022]. Available from: http://www.bristol.ac.uk/media-library/sites/geography/pfrc/Geography%20of%20gambling%20premises.pdf

- C, T. 2017. Untitled review on Pubs Galore. 21 September. [Accessed 10 July 2022] Available from:https://www.pubsgalore.co.uk/pubs/25380/

- Cumming, E. 2017. *How Britain fell for Wetherspoon's*. The Observer. [Online] 6 August. [Accessed 6 October 2022] Available from: https://www.theguardian.com/lifeandstyle/2017/aug/06/how-britain-fell-for-wetherspoons

- Darkest London. 2013. *Michael X and the Black House of Holloway Road*. [Online]. [Accessed 6 October 2022]. Available from: https://darkestlondon.com/tag/the-black-house/

- DHP Family. 2023. *Venue*. [Online]. [Accessed 24 April 2023]. Available from: https://www.dhpfamily.com/venues/

- Dimolderberg, A. 2022. *CHARLI XCX | CHICKEN SHOP DATE*. [Online video]. [Accessed 10 June 2022]. Available from: https://www.youtube.com/watch?v=bmX8pf5QIHM

- End of the Dialogue (Phelandaba). 1970. [Film]. Antonia Caccia & Simon Louvish. dir(s). UK: Icarus Films.

- Essential Living. 2022. *Vantage Point*. [Online]. [Accessed 6 October 2022]. Available from:https://www.essentialliving.co.uk/development/vantage-point/

- Ewan, R. 2012. *How to Make Archway Tower Disappear.* ['diminished reality' software viewed through a telescope and accompanying publication]. Central Saint Martins College of Arts & Design, London. Available at: http://www.ruthewan. com/wp-content/uploads/2017/02/How-to-Make-Archway-Tower-Disappear.pdf [Accessed 6 October 2022].

- Ferguson, S. 2020. Tavern's back! Archway pub reopens after 6-year closure saga. *Islington Tribune*. [Online]. 28 August. [Accessed 6 October 2022]. Available from:https://www.islingtontribune.co.uk/article/taverns-back-archway-pub-reopens-after-6-year-closure-saga

- Finch, E. 2017. Navigator Square – built on the pluck of the Irish. *Islington Tribune*. [Online]. 8 December. [Accessed 6 October 2022]. Available from:https://www. islingtontribune.co.uk/article/navigator-square-built-on-the-pluck-of-the-irish

- Finch, E. 2017. Squatters move into Holloway pub in rents protest. *Islington Tribune*. [Online]. 18 August. [Accessed 6 October 2022] Available from: https:// www.islingtontribune.co.uk/article/squatters-move-into-pub-in-rents-protest

- Flynn's Holloway. 2022. *WELCOME TO FLYNN'S*. [Online]. [Accessed 11 July 2022] Available from:https://www.flynnsholloway.co.uk/

- Gelder, S. 2018. Marks and Spencer in Holloway Road to close, Archway to get M&S Foodhall next year. *Islington Gazette*. [Online]. 22 May. [Accessed 6 October 2022]. Available from: https://www.islingtongazette.co.uk/news/marks-and-spencer-in-holloway-road-to-close-archway-to-3793058

- Gillman, P., Jones, C.. 1973. ON THE EDGE OF THE GHETTO: The way they see it. *The Sunday Times Magazine* [Online] 30 September. [Accessed 19 Janurary 2022]. Available from: https://archive.org/details/FCWFTimes/mode/2up

- Graty, C. 2010. *Making Inroads: A Story of Putting Down Roots on and Around the Holloway Road*. London: Rowan Arts.

- Hammerton. 2017. *HAMMERTON: PROUDLY BREWING GREAT BEER IN LONDON N7*. [Online]. [Accessed 6 October 2022] Available from: https://www. hammertonbrewery.co.uk/site/

- Hanly, C. 2018. Plans to turn The Archway Tavern into a wine bar AND nursery are rejected. *Hot Dinners*. [Online]. 23 August. [Accessed 6 October 2022]. Available from:https://www.hot-dinners.com/201808237548/Gastroblog/Latest-news/plans-to-turn-the-archway-tavern-into-a-wine-bar-and-nursery-are-rejected

- Harambee. 1969. [Publicity material (letters, flyers, leaflets and articles by Brother Herman, Secretary) and organisational material]. The Harambee Project Project, 1969, JLR/3/1/16. London: George Padmore Institute.
- Hidden London. 2022. *Archway, Islington*. [Online]. [Accessed 6 October 2022]. Available from:https://hidden-london.com/gazetteer/archway/
- Hussein, M. 2010. War on strip clubs in Islington. *Islington Gazette*. [Online]. 4 November. [Accessed 6 October 2022]. Available from: https://www.islingtongazette.co.uk/news/local-council/war-on-strip-clubs-in-islington-3679020
- Inge, S. 2016. The Quays pub, Holloway, to be refurbished and reopened. *Islington Gazette*. [Online]. 9 February. [Accessed 6 October 2022]. Available from:https://www.islingtongazette.co.uk/news/the-quays-pub-holloway-to-be-refurbished-and-reopened-3747834
- Islington. 2019. *Islington Local Plan Strategic and development management policies September 2019*. [Online]. [Accessed 6 October 2022]. Available from: https://bit.ly/3TPYCAD
- London Remembers. 2023. *Cromwell Road WW1 memorial*. [Online]. [Accessed 10 April 2023]. Available from: https://www.londonremembers.com/memorials/cromwell-road-ww1-memorial
- London Remembers. 2023. *Orbital*. [Online]. [Accessed 10 April 2023]. Available from: https://www.londonremembers.com/memorials/orbital
- McAllister, J. 2009. The Pub in Holloway. Beans On Toast. *Standing On A Chair*. [Digital]. London: Xtra Mile Recordings.
- Malakian, D., Odadjian, S., Tankia, S., and Dolmayan. J. 2001. Toxicity. System of a Down. *Toxicity*. [Digital]. Los Angeles: American Recordings, New York: Columbia Records.
- Marsh, A. 2023. Wetherspoons confirms sale of The Coronet pub in Holloway Road. *Islington Gazette*. [Online]. 23 August. [Accessed 21 December 2023]. Available from:https://www.islingtongazette.co.uk/news/23742466.wetherspoons-confirms-sale-coronet-pub-holloway-road/
- Marsh, A. 2023. Holloway Wetherspoon pub The Coronet to shut on December 10. *Islington Gazette*. [Online]. 30 November. [Accessed 21 December 2023]. Available from: https://www.islingtongazette.co.uk/news/23958767.holloway-wetherspoon-pub-coronet-shut-december-10/

- Meek, J. 1962. Telstar. The Tornados. *Telstar*. [Digital]. London: Decca.
- Morris, J. 2016. Justice for the Archway One! Arsenal fan Mick Doherty's Emirates ban lifted after four-year campaign. *Islington Gazette*. [Online]. 12 August. [Accessed 6 October 2022]. Available from: https://www.islingtongazette.co.uk/news/justice-for-the-archway-one-arsenal-fan-mick-doherty-s-3758002
- O'brien, J. 2022. Arsenal Fan TV's 'Mr DT' releases statement after being jailed for three years. *Mirror*. [Online] 20 January. [Accessed 6 October 2022]. Available from: https://www.mirror.co.uk/sport/football/news/arsenal-fan-tvs-mr-dt-26005724
- Oluwalana, A. 2022. Legendary North London Wetherspoons set to be sold off as locals fear 'old people will have nowhere to go'. *MyLondon*. [Online]. 25 November. [Accessed 24 April 2023]. Available from: https://www.mylondon.news/news/north-london-news/legendary-north-london-wetherspoons-set-25608368
- Owl & Hitchhiker. 2022. *WE LIVE AGAIN!!*. [Online]. [Accessed 6 October 2022]. Available from: https://www.owlandhitchhiker.pub/
- PubWiki. 2020. *Marlborough*. [Online]. [Accessed 23 October 2022]. Available from: https://pubwiki.co.uk/LondonPubs/Islington/Marlborough.shtml
- PubWiki. 2020. *Norfolk Arms, 557 Holloway Road, Islington N19*. [Online]. [Accessed 6 October 2022]. Available from:https://pubwiki.co.uk/LondonPubs/Hackney/NorfolkArms.shtml
- PubWiki. 2022. *Castle, 81 Holloway Road, Islington N7*. [Online]. [Accessed 6 October 2022]. Available from: https://pubwiki.co.uk/LondonPubs/Islington/Castle.shtml
- PubWiki. 2021. *Nags Head, 456 Holloway Road, Islington N1*. [Online]. [Accessed 6 October 2022]. Available from:https://pubwiki.co.uk/LondonPubs/Islington/NagsHeadHolloway.shtml
- Redmond, K. 2012. *Born and Bred: Stories of Holloway Road*. London: Rowan Arts.
- Reel, P. 1981. The Big Soundsystem Splash Down. New Musical Express. [Online]. 21 February. [Accessed 15 April 2023]. Available from: https://uncarved.org/dub/splash/index.html
- Reggae. 1971. [Film]. Horace Ové. dir. UK.
- samd_official. 2023. *They had so little booze left it was chaos RIP The Coronet*. [Online]. [11 December 2023]. Available from: https://vm.tiktok.com/ZGeNKm1E2/

- ScrapeHero. 2021. *Number of J D Wetherspoon Pubs locations in the UK in 2021*. [Online]. [Accessed 6 October 2022] Available from: https://www.scrapehero.com/location-reports/J%20D%20Wetherspoon%20Pubs-UK/

- setlist.fm. 2022. *May 13 2022 Frank Turner Setlist at Nambucca, London, England*. [Online]. [Accessed 24 April 2023]. Available from: https://www.setlist.fm/setlist/frank-turner/2022/nambucca-london-england-33b73069.html

- Stagedoor. 2017. *86 Holloway ABC 08*. [Flickr] 26 September. [Accessed 6 October 2022] Available from: https://www.flickr.com/photos/stagedoor/2138570478

- TFL. 2017. *Work to transform Archway town centre is complete*. [Online]. [Accessed 6 October 2022]. Available from:https://tfl.gov.uk/info-for/media/press-releases/2017/july/work-to-transform-archway-town-centre-is-complete

- *The Bank Job*. 2008. [Film]. Roger Donaldson. dir. UK: Mosaic Media Group, Relativity Media LLC, and Skyline Productions.

- The Diary of Samuel Pepys. 2022. *Tuesday 24 September 1661*. [Online]. [Accessed 6 October 2022]. Available from:https://www.pepysdiary.com/diary/1661/09/24/

- The Garage. 2023. Go_A. [Online]. [Accessed 24 April 2023] Available from: https://www.thegarage.london/gigs/go_a-the-garage-london-tickets-2022/

- The Intrepid Fox. 2015. *THE INTREPID FOX's view from the bar…"deus ex machina" (16/3/15)*. [Facebook]. 16 March. [Accessed 6 October 2022]. Available from:https://bit.ly/3TKJV1P

- The Kinks. *Muswell Hillbillies*. 1971. [Vinyl]. London: RCA.

- The Labour Party. 2017. *FOR THE MANY NOT THE FEW: THE LABOUR PARTY MANIFESTO 2017*. [Online]. [Accessed 6 October 2022]. Available from: https://labour.org.uk/wp-content/uploads/2017/10/labour-manifesto-2017.pdf

- The Spoke. 2022. *HOME*. [Online]. [Accessed 23 October 2022] Available from: http://www.thespokelondon.com/

- Tramway Information. 2002. *Highgate Hill Cable Tramway, Car 9*. [Online]. [Accessed 6 October 2022]. Available from:https://www.tramwayinfo.com/Tramframe.htm?

- True Pub Co. 2022. *ABOUT US*. [Online]. [Accessed 6 October 2022] Available from:https://www.truepubco.co.uk/about/

- Turner, F. 2007. The Ballad of Me and My Friends. Frank Turner. *Sleep Is for the Week*. [Digital]. London: Xtra Mile Recordings.

- WhatPub. 2021. *Bailey*. [Online]. [Accessed 6 October 2022]. Available from:https://whatpub.com/pubs/NLD/5680/bailey-holloway
- WhatPub. 2021. *Gaff*. [Online]. [Accessed 6 October 2022]. Available from: https://whatpub.com/pubs/NLD/5658/gaff-holloway
- WhatPub. 2021. *Lion*. [Online]. [Accessed 6 October 2022]. Available from: https://whatpub.com/pubs/NLD/5872/lion-upper-holloway
- WhatPub. 2022. *Big Red*. [Online]. [Accessed 6 October 2022]. Available from:https://whatpub.com/pubs/NLD/5642/big-red-holloway
- WhatPub. 2022. *House of Hammerton*. [Online]. [Accessed 6 October 2022]. Available from:https://whatpub.com/pubs/NLD/5679/house-of-hammerton-holloway
- WhatPub. 2022. *Islington Sports Bar*. [Online]. [Accessed 6 October 2022]. Available from:https://whatpub.com/pubs/NLD/5656/islington-sports-bar-holloway
- WhatPub. 2022. *Nambucca*. [Online]. [Accessed 6 October 2022]. Available from:https://whatpub.com/pubs/NLD/5655/nambucca-holloway
- WhatPub. 2023. *Arkstar*. [Online]. [Accessed 24 April 2023]. Available from: https://whatpub.com/pubs/NLD/16957/arkstar-holloway
- Yelp. 2010. *Dusk Till Dawn*. [Online]. [Accessed 6 October 2022]. Available from:https://www.yelp.com/biz/dusk-till-dawn-london

Terminus

Thank you Maggie, Holloway Crawl's protagonist, for letting me embarrass you and for being soft with me during my deranged spells of spouting mostly useless and completely unsolicited Holloway facts.

Thank you Aline and Millie for proofing and convincing me of Holloway Crawl's successes. This getting released in any form is completely your fault.

Thank you Dr Ben Bethell, my MA dissertation tutor, for helping shape the early versions of this research project when it was just a poorly researched dissertation. Your wisdom is invaluable to me and I really hope you like what is now a poorly researched activity book.

Thank you Mum for shepherding me and my stuff down Holloway Road every time I needed you to, and for always being my biggest cheerleader.

And to Russell, to Sheldon, to the participants of every overheard conversation, to the women that called us disgusting, to the lads who took the piss out of my mullet, to every bartender, to every person that populated and defined this project by making my experience of Holloway Road what it has been, and to all the people of Holloway and its adjacent areas, named or otherwise: thank you. I love it here.